THIS BOOK BELONGS TO:

The Red Headed Hostess

"Being the hostess to your own life and family"

© The Red Headed Hostess

TABLE OF CONTENTS

TABLE OF CONTENTS

TABLE OF CONTENTS: Virtue Project

HOW DO I USE THIS JOURNAL?

About this journal:

This journal is designed to help you get the most out of your Personal Progress goals and to have fun while doing it! Each experience is carefully designed to help you accomplish the required and optional experiences in your Personal Progress program, and to truly have progress in your life as you work through them.

What is doodling?

As you are studying scriptures and other references, doodle what you are learning on the pages. For example, you can doodle your favorite quotes, phrases and scriptures. You can add pictures, diagrams, stickers, glue things on – whatever you would like! Each doodle journal should be as unique and different as the girls filling them out.

Are there examples I can look at?

Yes. Come to **www.theredheadedhostess.com** and click on "books" in the upper right corner. Find this book and click on "examples".

Do I have to do every experience?

Follow the guidelines in your Personal Progress book to know what experiences are required and which ones are optional.

Should I look up every reference and scripture suggested?

The references come from the Personal Progress program and were chosen and approved of carefully by your leaders. Take time to consider each one and to record what you learned from them. If you have trouble understanding some of them, ask your parents, leaders or someone for help.

What if I need more room to write or doodle?

It is very likely that you will have so much to write or draw that you will need more room. Simply get a piece of paper, finish your thoughts and tape or glue it in. You can use a cute paper from a note pad or lined paper like you use in school. You may want to trim down the paper so it fits well inside of your book. You can tape it along the top, or into the creases of the pages so your added paper will turn like a page.

What do I do on the challenge pages?

Throughout the personal progress book there are several times you are asked to work on something for a number of weeks. These challenge pages are so you can keep track of your progress and report back to yourself as you work on them. As you fill in these pages and work on these challenges you should see real and positive changes in your life, or rather you should see in yourself *personal progress*.

What should I do on the Book of Mormon doodle pages?

As you fulfill your virtue project and study the Book of Mormon, use these pages to doodle your favorite scriptures and phrases. You could also doodle pictures of the stories, timelines, people, things you are learning and loving, definitions of words you looked up, reviews of what you read, etc.

DOODLING IDEAS

ADD DESIGNS TO THE TITLE

Draw frames around things

ADD CUTE ARROWS

Draw in pencil first and then trace with a pen

Vary your handwriting

SIZE & STYLE

Empasize the first letter

PICK A COLOR THEME FOR A PAGE

Draw Borders

Add cute punctuations

use cute lettering

Draw a box around a word

Add Doodles!

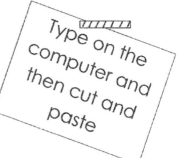

Type on the computer and then cut and paste

Fill this page with doodles of all the **QUOTES** and **SCRIPTURES** you can find about **FAITH.**   Be certain to include the saying about this value in your Personal Progress booklet.

ALMA 32:17-43

As you study these **SCRIPTURES,** doodle what you learn about **FAITH.** Include your own thoughts and insights, definitions, pictures, etc.

HEBREWS 11

As you study this chapter, grab a **DICTIONARY** and use it to look up words you do not understand. Doodle the words and definitions all over the top half of this page.

Doodle what you learn about **FAITH** on the bottom half of this page.

Joseph Smith History 1:11-20

11 While I was laboring under the extreme difficulties caused by the contests of these parties of religionists, I was one day reading the *Making a great effort* Epistle of James, first chapter and fifth verse, which reads: *If any of you lack wisdom, let him ask of God, that giveth to all men liberally, and upbraideth not; and it shall be given him.*

12 Never did any passage of scripture come with more power to the heart of man than this did at this time to mine. It seemed to enter with great force into every feeling of my heart. I reflected on it again and again, knowing that if any person needed wisdom from God, I did; for how to act I did not know, and unless I could get more wisdom than I then had, I would never know; for the teachers of religion of the different sects understood the same passages of scripture so differently as to destroy all confidence in settling the question by an appeal to the Bible.

13 At length I came to the conclusion that I must either remain in darkness and confusion, or else I must do as James directs, that is, ask of God. I at length came to the determination to "ask of God," concluding that if he gave wisdom to them that lacked wisdom, and would give liberally, and not upbraid, I might venture.

14 So, in accordance with this, my determination to ask of God, I retired to the woods to make the attempt. It was on the morning of a beautiful, clear day, early in the spring of eighteen hundred and twenty. It was the first time in my life that I had made such an attempt, for amidst all my anxieties I had never as yet made the attempt to pray vocally.

15 After I had retired to the place where I had previously designed to go, having looked around me, and finding myself alone, I kneeled down and began to offer up the desires of my heart to God. I had scarcely done so, when immediately I was seized upon by some power which entirely overcame me, and had such an astonishing influence over me as to bind my tongue so that I could not speak. Thick darkness gathered around me, and it seemed to me for a time as if I were doomed to sudden destruction.

Faith #1

16 But, exerting all my powers to call upon God to deliver me out of the power of this enemy which had seized upon me, and at the very moment when I was ready to sink into despair and abandon myself to destruction—not to an imaginary ruin, but to the power of some actual being from the unseen world, who had such marvelous power as I had never before felt in any being—just at this moment of great alarm, I saw a pillar of light exactly over my head, above the brightness of the sun, which descended gradually until it fell upon me.

17 It no sooner appeared than I found myself delivered from the enemy which held me bound. When the light rested upon me I saw two Personages, whose brightness and glory defy all description, standing above me in the air. One of them spake unto me, calling me by name and said, pointing to the other—*This is My Beloved Son. Hear Him!*

18 My object in going to inquire of the Lord was to know which of all the sects was right, that I might know which to join. No sooner, therefore, did I get possession of myself, so as to be able to speak, than I asked the Personages who stood above me in the light, which of all the sects was right (for at this time it had never entered into my heart that all were wrong)—and which I should join.

19 I was answered that I must join none of them, for they were all wrong; and the Personage who addressed me said that all their creeds were an abomination in his sight; that those professors were all corrupt; that: "they draw near to me with their lips, but their hearts are far from me, they teach for doctrines the commandments of men, having a form of godliness, but they deny the power thereof."

20 He again forbade me to join with any of them; and many other things did he say unto me, which I cannot write at this time. When I came to myself again, I found myself lying on my back, looking up into heaven. When the light had departed, I had no strength; but soon recovering in some degree, I went home. And as I leaned up to the fireplace, mother inquired what the matter was. I replied, "Never mind, all is well—I am well enough off." I then said to my mother, "I have learned for myself that Presbyterianism is not true." It seems as though the adversary was aware, at a very early period of my life, that I was destined to prove a disturber and an annoyer of his kingdom; else why should the powers of darkness combine against me? Why the opposition and persecution that arose against me, almost in my infancy?

Now go back and highlight the phrases that teach you something about FAITH.

11

Faith #1

ETHER 12:6-22

Doodle your favorite **PHRASES** from these verses on this page

Faith #1

Find 2 General
Conference talks
about

FAITH.

Doodle your
favorite quotes
and your
personal
thoughts on
these next two
pages.

Title of talk #1:

Speaker:

Date given:

Title of talk #2:

Speaker:

Date given:

Faith #1

BUILDING MY FAITH
Through Daily Prayer

For the next 21 days (three weeks) say your morning and evening prayers every day. During and at the end of this experience doodle (on the next page) how having meaningful, daily prayers is building your faith.

DAY 1	DAY 2	DAY 3
Date: ☐ Morning ☐ Evening	Date: ☐ Morning ☐ Evening	Date: ☐ Morning ☐ Evening
DAY 4	**DAY 5**	**DAY 6**
Date: ☐ Morning ☐ Evening	Date: ☐ Morning ☐ Evening	Date: ☐ Morning ☐ Evening
DAY 7	**DAY 8**	**DAY 9**
Date: ☐ Morning ☐ Evening	Date: ☐ Morning ☐ Evening	Date: ☐ Morning ☐ Evening
DAY 10	**DAY 11**	**DAY 12**
Date: ☐ Morning ☐ Evening	Date: ☐ Morning ☐ Evening	Date: ☐ Morning ☐ Evening
DAY 13	**DAY 14**	**DAY 15**
Date: ☐ Morning ☐ Evening	Date: ☐ Morning ☐ Evening	Date: ☐ Morning ☐ Evening
DAY 16	**DAY 17**	**DAY 18**
Date: ☐ Morning ☐ Evening	Date: ☐ Morning ☐ Evening	Date: ☐ Morning ☐ Evening
DAY 19	**DAY 20**	**DAY 21**
Date: ☐ Morning ☐ Evening	Date: ☐ Morning ☐ Evening	Date: ☐ Morning ☐ Evening

Doodle your thoughts about how saying your morning and evening prayers every day is building your faith.

HOW DAILY PRAYER
is building my faith

ALMA 56:45-48 & 57:21

Read these verses, and then WRITE A LETTER to the mothers of the stripling warriors about what they taught you about Motherhood & Faith.

Faith #2

Have your **MOTHER, GRANDMOTHER,** or Mother you admire write YOU a letter about their experience with FAITH and MOTHERHOOD and how you can prepare yourself for that important role.

MOTHERHOOD

Read **THE FAMILY: A PROCLAMATION TO THE WORLD**. Doodle everything you learn about Motherhood all over this page.

Faith #2

MY THOUGHTS ON MOTHERHOOD

Record your personal thoughts and feelings of Motherhood.

Look up

FAITH in your **Bible Dictionary**. Doodle the things you learn, including: words, phrases, quotes, scriptures, pictures, diagrams and personal thoughts.

Look up **FAITH** in True to the Faith. Doodle the things you learn, including: words, phrases, quotes, scriptures, pictures, diagrams and personal thoughts.

Ask **A FAMILY MEMBER** to write you a letter about an experience that has strengthened his or her faith.

Faith #3

Write about **AN EXPERIENCE OF YOUR OWN** that has strengthened your *faith*.

Faith #3

Plan a Family Home Evening

Choose any Gospel Principle (you can look through *True to the Faith* or the *For the Strength of Youth* pamphlet to choose one). Teach your family how FAITH can help you live that Gospel principle.

GOSPEL PRINCIPLE : _____

A fun idea to get my family excited for the lesson (something I can do earlier in the day or week):	A fun, interesting or engaging way I can introduce the topic to my family:
An activity or discussion my family can have (or do) to learn more about FAITH and this principle:	What we can do to apply what we have learned to our lives:

How the Sacrament Increases My FAITH

Read the following three accounts of **THE LAST SUPPER.** Doodle things you learn (what happened, who was there, words you looked up, pictures, etc.) in each column.

Matthew 26:26-28   ## Mark 14:22-24   ## Luke 22:17-20

The Sacrament

Look through the
SACRAMENT HYMNS
and doodle some of
your favorite phrases
on this page.

Faith #4

Study the Sacrament prayer in **D&C 20:75-79**. Doodle the promises you make and the blessings you receive in each prayer. Look up "Sacrament" in *True to the Faith* for additional insights.

BREAD

WATER

How the Sacrament Increases my Faith

For three weeks make a special effort to listen carefully to the Sacrament Hymns and think about why we partake of the bread and water. After three weeks record how studying about the Sacrament and making a careful effort during the Sacrament has influenced you.

My Faith
and the
ATONEMENT

Look up the following scriptures below. Use this page for DEFINTIONS you look up.

Use the other page to doodle everything you are learning about the Atonement from the scriptures.

Isaiah 53:3-12

John 3:16-17

Romans 5

2 Nephi 9:6-7

2 Nephi 9:21-26

Alma 7:11-13

Alma 34:8-17

D&C 19:15-20

Bible Dictionary:
Atonement

The ATONEMENT of Jesus Christ

Quotes about the ATONEMENT of Jesus Christ

Fill this page with your favorite General Conference quotes about the Atonement.

Faith #5

MY FEELINGS

Record your personal feelings about the Savior, His Atonement and what He has done for you.

_____
_____
_____
_____
_____
_____
_____
_____
_____
_____
_____
_____
_____
_____
_____
_____
_____
_____
_____
_____
_____
_____
_____
_____
_____
_____
_____
_____

My Faith and the PLAN OF SALVATION

Here is a basic outline of the Plan of Salvation. Label it as best as you can. Then look up the scriptures down the side of the page and doodle all over these pages things you learn about The Plan — you can also doodle great quotes you find!

Revelation 12:7-9

1 Corinthians 15:22

2 Nephi 9:1-28

2 Nephi 11:4-7

D&C 76:50-113

D&C 93:33-34

Moses 4:1-4

Abraham 3:24-27

"Plan of Salvation" in *True to the Faith*

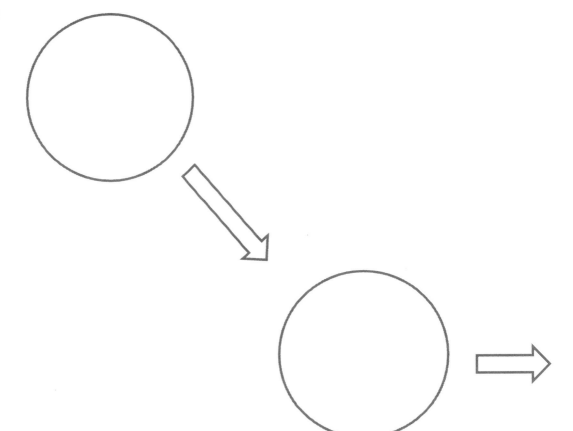

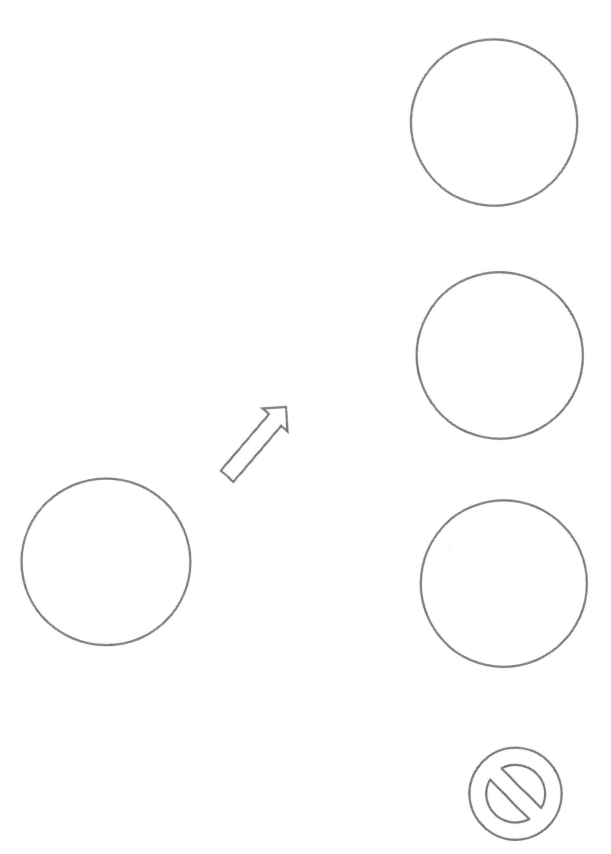

Faith #6

The PLAN OF SALVATION & ME

How has your knowledge of the Plan of Salvation impacted your actions?

How has your knowledge of the Plan of Salvation helped you understand your identity?

How has your knowledge of the Plan of Salvation strengthened your faith?

My Faith and TITHING

Look up the following scriptures. Pick your favorite PHRASE and doodle it on this page. Include pictures if you like.

D&C 119
MALACHI 3:8-12

Faith #7

Record on this page how paying your

TITHING

has helped your faith grow.

List all of the blessings you can think
of that have come to you and your
family because you live the law of

TITHING.

Faith #7

My Project

For my project I have chosen to:

_____
_____
_____
_____
_____
_____
_____

BRAINSTORM

As many ideas as you can to help you have an impactful and successful project.

What I hope to gain from this project:

_____
_____
_____
_____
_____
_____
_____

A report of my project (including specifics of what I did and what I learned):

_____

_____

_____

_____

_____

_____

_____

_____

_____

_____

_____

_____

_____

_____

_____

_____

_____

_____

_____

_____

_____

_____

_____

_____

_____

_____

_____

_____

_____

_____

Faith Project

DIVINE NATURE

Fill this page with doodles of all the **QUOTES** and **SCRIPTURES** you can find about **DIVINE NATURE.** Be certain to include the saying about this value in your Personal Progress booklet.

WHAT ARE THE DIVINE QUALITIES
of a Daughter of God ?

Look up all of the references on this page. Doodle every **DIVINE QUALITY** you can find.

2 Peter 1

Alma 7:23-24

D&C 121:45

The Family: A Proclamation to the World

Divine Nature #1

DEVELOPING MY DIVINE QUALITIES

Look at each **DIVINE QUALITY** you recorded on the last page. Consider what you can do to develop those qualities in yourself.

Quality	How I can develop this quality

43

WOMANHOOD

As a young woman, you have **DIVINE FEMININE QUALITIES.** Study the following references that teach you about those qualities and doodle what you learn on this page.

PROVERBS 31:10-31

THE FAMILY A PROCLAMATION TO THE WORLD
(specifically what it says about being a wife and mother)

Find 2 General Conference talks about

WOMANHOOD.

Doodle your favorite quotes and your personal thoughts on these next two pages.

Title of talk #1:

Speaker:

Date given:

Divine Nature #2

Title of talk #2:

Speaker:

Date given:

Divine Nature #2

IMPORTANT ATTRIBUTES of a *Mother*

Ask your mother or another woman in your life to write you a letter and share a list of important attributes for being a mother.

_____

_____

_____

_____

_____

_____

_____

_____

_____

_____

_____

_____

_____

_____

_____

_____

_____

_____

_____

_____

_____

_____

_____

_____

_____

_____

_____

_____

_____

_____

Divine Nature #2

Choose one of the attributes (from the letter written to you) that you would like to develop in yourself. Write it here:

ATTRIBUTE: --

Doodle all of the ideas you can think of for how you can develop this attribute. Think of both big and small things.

Work on developing this attribute. Make your own plan and goals of what you are going to do and how long you are going to work on it. Draw out your plan here.

2 WEEK CHALLENGE: Making My Home Life Better

For two weeks do all you can to strengthen your relationships in your family. In the boxes below, make notes about the details of each time you did these things during the 2 weeks. Review what you have done each night and plan out things you can do the next day. Try to do each thing multiple times and fill these pages up as much as possible.

I didn't criticize:	I gave a meaningful compliment

I wrote a note of encouragement	I expressed gratitude

I spoke kindly rather than unkindly	I looked for good qualities in others

Divine Nature #3

I found a way to be helpful	I did a secret act of service
I apologized	I prayed, specifically, for a family member
I was patient and understanding	I expressed love in word or action
I surprised someone with something nice	I noticed when someone needed love

Divine Nature #3

2 WEEK CHALLENGE: Making My Home Life Better

REPORT

What was your favorite experience of the two weeks?

_____
_____
_____
_____
_____
_____
_____
_____
_____
_____
_____
_____

What positive and divine qualities did you notice in your family as you served them?

_____
_____
_____
_____
_____
_____
_____
_____
_____
_____
_____
_____

How did this experience help prepare you for your role of a wife and mother?

_____
_____
_____
_____
_____
_____
_____
_____
_____
_____
_____

What divine qualities did you notice in yourself the past two weeks?

_____
_____
_____
_____
_____
_____
_____
_____
_____
_____
_____

THE SACRAMENT PRAYERS & Me

Study the sacrament prayers in D&C 20:77 and 79. Look up at least 10 words in the dictionary. Doodle their **DEFINITIONS** in this space.

MEMORIZE

Work on memorizing the sacrament prayers. Start by trying to fill in the blanks:

DOCTRINE & COVENANTS 20:77

O God, the _____ Father, we _____ thee in the _____ of thy Son, Jesus Christ, to _____ and sanctify this _____ to the _____ of all those who partake of it, that they may _____ in remembrance of the body of thy _____, and _____ unto thee, O God, the Eternal Father, that they are willing to take upon them the _____ of thy Son, and always _____ him and keep his _____ which he has given them; that they may _____ have his _____ to be with them. Amen.

DOCTRINE & COVENANTS 20:77

O God, the _____ Father, we _____ thee in the _____ of thy Son, Jesus Christ, to bless and _____ this _____ to the souls of all those who _____ of it, that they _____ do it in _____ of the _____ of thy Son, which was _____ for them; that they may witness unto _____, O God, the Eternal Father, that they do _____ remember him, that they may have his _____ to be with them. _____.

53

Divine Nature #4

MEMORIZE THE SACRAMENT PRAYERS

Here are the first letters of each word for the scriptures that contain the sacrament prayers. See if you can write out the scriptures correctly. After you finish, look up the scripture and check what you have written.

DOCTRINE & COVENANTS 20:77

O G. t E F, w a t i t n o t S, J C, t b a s t b t t s o a t w p o i, t t m e i r o t b o t S, a w u t, O G, t E F, t t a w t t u t t n o t S, a a r h a k h c w h h g t; t t m a h h S t b w t. A.

DOCTRINE & COVENANTS 20:79

O G. t E F, w a t i t n o t S, J C, t b a s t w t t s o a t w d o i, t t m d i i r o t b o t S, w w s f t; t t m w u t, O G, t E F, t t d a r h, t t m h h S t b w t. A.

Below are the beginning of phrases from the Sacrament Prayers. See if you can complete each phrase up until the point where the next phrase begins.

DOCTRINE & COVENANTS 20:77

O God,
We ask the in the
To bless and
To the souls of all
That they may eat
Of thy Son, and
O God,
That they are willing to
The name
And always
And keep
Which he has
That they may
To be

DOCTRINE & COVENANTS 20:77

O God,
We ask thee
To bless and
To the souls of
That they may
Of the
Which was
That they may
O God,
That they do
That they may
To be

Divine Nature #4

MY BAPTISMAL COVENANT

Taking Upon the Name of Jesus Christ

Keeping the Commandments

Serving the Lord

 You made a covenant with God when you were baptized and you renew that covenant each time you partake of the

SACRAMENT.

Look up "Baptism" in True to the Faith, and find the section titled. "Your Baptismal Covenant". Doodle what you learn in the proper spaces.

How can developing your divine qualities help you fulfill your covenant to "take upon the name of Jesus Christ"?

_____

_____

_____

_____

_____

_____

OBEDIENCE

Look up
LUKE 2:40-51
and
JOHN 6:38
Doodle what you learn
about "obedience".

Look up in
THE FAMILY: A PROCLAMATION OF THE WORLD
Doodle what you learn
about the
divine roles
of **MOTHERS** and **FATHERS**.

2 WEEK CHALLENGE: Obeying & Honoring
My Parent's Divine Roles

After studying the Savior's example of obedience and your parent's divine roles, spend two weeks putting forth a special effort in treating your parents with respect and kindness and doing what they ask without being asked. At the end of each day record what you did that day to obey and honor them and their divine roles.

DAY 1   DATE:

What I did today to honor and obey my parents:

_____

_____

_____

_____

What I did without being asked:

_____

_____

_____

DAY 2   DATE:

What I did today to honor and obey my parents:

_____

_____

_____

_____

How I showed gratitude to my parents:

_____

_____

_____

DAY 3   DATE:

What I did today to honor and obey my parents:

_____

_____

_____

_____

What divine roles I saw my parents fulfill:

_____

_____

_____

DAY 4   DATE:

What I did today to honor and obey my parents:

_____

_____

_____

_____

Some kind things I said to my parents:

_____

_____

_____

DAY 5   DATE:

What I did today to honor and obey my parents:

_____

_____

_____

_____

What I did today without being asked:

_____

_____

_____

DAY 6   DATE:

What I did today to honor and obey my parents:

_____

_____

_____

_____

How I expressed gratitude to my parents:

_____

_____

_____

Divine Nature #5

DAY 7   DATE:

What I did today to honor and obey my parents:

_____
_____
_____
_____

What divine roles I saw my parents fulfill:

_____
_____
_____
_____

DAY 8   DATE:

What I did today to honor and obey my parents:

_____
_____
_____
_____

Kind things I said to my parents today:

_____
_____
_____
_____

DAY 9   DATE:

What I did today to honor and obey my parents:

_____
_____
_____
_____

I helped my parents fulfill their divine roles by:

_____
_____
_____
_____

DAY 10   DATE:

What I did today to honor and obey my parents:

_____
_____
_____
_____

What I did today without being asked:

_____
_____
_____
_____

DAY 11   DATE:

What I did today to honor and obey my parents:

_____
_____
_____
_____

What divine roles I saw my parents fulfill:

_____
_____
_____
_____

DAY 12   DATE:

What I did today to honor and obey my parents:

_____
_____
_____
_____

I helped my parents fulfill their divine roles by:

_____
_____
_____
_____

DAY 13   DATE:

What I did today to honor and obey my parents:

_____

_____

_____

_____

Kind things I said to my parents today:

_____

_____

_____

_____

DAY 14   DATE:

What I did today to honor and obey my parents:

_____

_____

_____

_____

What divine roles I saw my parents fulfill:

_____

_____

_____

_____

REPORT

What did you learn about your parent's divine roles these past two weeks?

_____

_____

_____

_____

_____

What divine roles did you observe that you would like to develop in yourself?

_____

_____

_____

_____

_____

How did being so obedient and respectful influence you, your parents and your entire family?

_____

_____

_____

_____

_____

_____

DEVELOPING MY Divine Qualities

Look up the following scriptures. Doodle all of the **DIVINE QUALITIES** mentioned in them.

Matthew 5:9

John 15:12

Galatians 5:22-23

Colossians 3:12-17

1 John 4:21

Moroni 7:44-48

Divine Nature #6

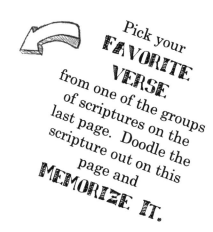

Pick your **FAVORITE VERSE** from one of the groups of scriptures on the last page. Doodle the scripture out on this page and **MEMORIZE IT.**

PICK ONE of the **DIVINE QUALITIES** from those scriptures and spend 2 weeks doing all you can to develop that divine quality.

QUALITY I CHOOSE:

BRAINSTORM everything you could do to develop this quality. Think of as many things as possible.

	DATE	WHAT I DID TO DEVELOP THIS QUALITY
Day #1		
Day #2		
Day #3		
Day #4		
Day #5		
Day #6		
Day #7		
Day #8		
Day #9		
Day #10		
Day #11		
Day #12		
Day #13		

Divine Nature #6

Being a *Peacemaker*

Learn the **DEFINITION** of "Peacemaker" and doodle it here.

Find **5 SCRIPTURES** that teach you about peacemakers and doodle what they teach you (be sure to include the references).

For TWO WEEKS focus on being a Peacemaker. Make a special effort to not complain, criticize or speak unkindly to others. Each night come to this page and doodle your experiences. Make your own calendar to report on, or draw numbers 1-14 (one number for each day of the challenge) on this page with space to write next to each number.

REPORT:
What did you earn and what special experiences did you have these past two weeks?

Why is being a
PEACEMAKER
An important part of your divine nature?

My Project

For my project I have chosen to:

BRAINSTORM
As many ideas as you can to help you have an impactful and successful project.

What I hope to gain from this project:

A report of my project (including specifics of what I did and what I learned):

Divine Nature Project

INDIVIDUAL
WORTH

Fill this page with doodles of all the **QUOTES** and **SCRIPTURES** you can find about **INDIVIDUAL WORTH.** Be certain to include the saying about this value in your Personal Progress booklet.

I AM A Daughter of ....

Heavenly Father

Study these scriptures and doodle what they teach you about how much **HEAVENLY FATHER** loves you, knows you, And is mindful of you

Psalm 8:4-6

Jeremiah 1:5

John 13:34

D&C 18:10

Abraham 3:22-23

Joseph Smith History 1:1-20

PATRIARCHAL BLESSINGS

Study "PATRIARCHAL BLESSINGS" in *True to the Faith*. Doodle what you learn on this page.

Go to www.lds.org and search "PATRIARCHAL BLESSINGS" in the search bar. Refine your search by clicking on "General Conference" to the left. Find some good quotes about "Patriarchal Blessings" and write them on this page.

Individual Worth #2

Have a parent or other important adult in your life write you a letter with counsel to you about how to prepare for your Patriarchal Blessing (if you have not yet received it) and how to use it as a light and guide in your life.

Individual Worth #2

Individual Worth
IN OTHERS

Look up the
following
scriptures and
doodle what they
teach you about
the
**WORTH IN
OTHERS.**

D&C 18:10

D&C 121:45

2 WEEK CHALLENGE:
Seeing Other's Individual Worth

For two weeks make a special effort to notice the good qualities in others. Pray each day for help in recognizing them. Seek to notice them in your family, friends, and others in your life. At the end of each day write down the qualities you noticed.

DATE		QUALITIES I NOTICED IN OTHERS
Day #1		
Day #2		
Day #3		
Day #4		
Day #5		
Day #6		
Day #7		

Individual Worth #3

Day #8		
Day #9		
Day #10		
Day #11		
Day #12		
Day #13		
Day #14		

What did this experience teach you?

Individual Worth #3

ORGANIZE YOURSELF

Look up
D&C 88:119
and doodle what
it teaches you
about this title.

Doodle all of your
hopes and dreams for
your future. Include
your desires for

Your future family

MARRIAGE

EDUCATION

HOME

Role as a mother

Things you would like
to accomplish

Etc.

Individual Worth #4

ORGANIZE YOURSELF
BY Making a Plan

Make a plan on how to make your hopes and dreams a reality. List your hopes on the left and detailed plans to the right. If you need more pages continue writing on smaller paper and then tape them onto this page.

HOPES & DREAMS	MY PLAN

Individual Worth #4

INCREASING MY SELF-CONFIDENCE

Participate in some public performance or activity (a dance, speech, giving a lesson, music performance, drama, etc.) It can be at school, church or the community. Record what you did and how it influenced your self-confidence.

Individual Worth #5

Visit with your relatives and find out as much about your ancestors as possible. Doodle what you learn on this page.

Family History

Go to www.lds.org and in the search bar put "pedigree chart". Find and then print one off. With the help of relatives, fill out the chart and then tape it onto this page.

How does understanding your family history help you understand your identity and individual worth?

Individual Worth #6

MY SPECIAL GIFTS

 Read these scriptures and
doodle on this page what you
learn about gifts that
Heavenly Father gives us.

1 Corinthians 12:4-12

Moroni 7:12-13

Moroni 10:8-18

D&C 46:11-26

Ask a family member, or someone close to you, to write down the positive qualities and special gifts they have observed in you.

_____

_____

_____

_____

_____

_____

_____

_____

_____

_____

_____

_____

Write how you are going to continue developing and using the gifts that your family member wrote above.

_____

_____

_____

_____

_____

_____

_____

_____

_____

_____

_____

_____

Individual Worth #7

My Project

For my project I have chosen to:

_____

_____

_____

_____

_____

_____

_____

BRAINSTORM
As many ideas as you can to help you have an impactful and successful project.

What I hope to gain from this project:

_____

_____

_____

_____

_____

_____

_____

A report of my project (including specifics of what I did and what I learned):

_____

_____

_____

_____

_____

_____

_____

_____

_____

_____

_____

_____

_____

_____

_____

_____

_____

_____

_____

_____

_____

_____

_____

_____

_____

_____

_____

_____

_____

_____

Individual Worth Project

KNOWLEDGE

Fill this page with doodles of all the **QUOTES** and **SCRIPTURES** you can find about **KNOWLEDGE.**
Be certain to include the saying about this value in your Personal Progress booklet.

THE IMPORTANCE OF GAINING KNOWLEDGE

Read these scriptures and doodle on this page what you learn about the importance of gaining knowledge.

Proverbs 1:5

Proverbs 4:7

2 Nephi 28:30

D&C 88:78-80

D&C 118

D&C 90:15

D&C 130:18-19

D&C 131:6

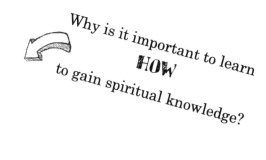

Why is it important to learn **HOW** to gain spiritual knowledge?

Why is it important to learn how to take the spiritual knowledge you gain and **APPLY** it to your present and future home and family life?

87

Knowledge #1

My Talents

Read the parable in MATTHEW 25:14-30.

Doodle that parable on this page.

Knowledge #2

MY TALENTS

Doodle **TALENTS** that you have and some you would like to develop.

SKILL:

Learn **A NEW SKILL** or talent that will help you in your future role as wife and mother.

Why have you chosen this skill? Why do you think it will bless your future family?

Make a plan of how you are going to learn this new skill or talent.

After you have learned this new skill, record your experience here:

We Seek After these Things

Work on memorizing the thirteenth Article of Faith. Start by reading the scripture several times and then trying to fill in the blanks without looking at your scriptures.

ARTICLE OF FAITH #13

We believe in being _____, true, _____, benevolent, _____, and in doing _____ to all men; indeed, we may say that we _____ the admonition of _____—We believe all _____, we _____ all things, we have _____ many things, and _____ to be able to endure all things. If there is anything virtuous, _____, or of good _____ or praiseworthy, we _____ after these things.

These are the first letters of each word in the Article of Faith. See if you can write it out correctly. After you finish look up the scripture and check what you have written.

ARTICLE OF FAITH #13

W b i b h, t, c, b, v, a i d g t a m ;
i, w m s t w f t a o P – W b a t, w h
a t, w h e m t, a h t b a t e a t. I t i
a v, l, o o g r o p, w s a t t.

➡

Below are the beginning of phrases from the thirteenth Article of Faith. See if you can complete each phrase up until the point where the next phrase begins.

We believe in being

Indeed, we may say

We believe all

And hope to be able

If there is anything

We seek

Seeking After these Things

Visit a museum or exhibit, or attend a performance. Evaluate what you saw and heard by using the thirteenth Article of Faith as your guide.

How can you use the thirteenth Article of Faith as a guide in all your future forms of entertainment?

Knowledge #3

GAINING SPIRITUAL KNOWLEDGE

Select a GOSPEL DOCTRINE or PRINCIPLE that you would like to learn more about (for example, faith, charity, repentance, prayer, etc.)

Write the doctrine or principle you chose in the center of this page.

Doodle all over this page and pack it as full as possible with scriptures, quotes, stories, etc. about the doctrine or principle you chose.

Knowledge #4

Write a 5 minute talk sharing what you learned about the Gospel or Principle you studied on the last page.

Knowledge #4

Gaining knowledge
of WORK or SERVICE

Learn about an area of **WORK** or **SERVICE** that you are interested in. Talk to someone who works or serves in that area. Find out the following things and doodle them on this page:

Their responsibilities

Necessary training

HOW THEIR JOB CONTRIBUTES TO SOCIETY

HYMNS

Select two of your favorite hymns. Doodle your favorite phrases as well as what the scriptures at the bottom of the hymn teaches you.

Hymn title #1: _____

- -

Hymn title #2: _____

- -

* Memorize both of those hymns and then learn how to properly conduct them. Find an opportunity to conduct them in a church meeting or in Family Home Evening.

GAINING KNOWLEDGE
of **Emergency** and **Survival Skills**

Review and doodle the **FIRST AID, SAFETY, SANITATION & SURVIVAL SKILLS** in your Young Women Camp Manual. (You can find it on www.lds.org if you click on "Resources", then "Young Women", then "Leader Resources", and then "Young Women Camp".

Also doodle a list of **BASIC SUPPLIES** your family may need in the case of an emergency.

My Project

For my project I have chosen to:

_____

_____

_____

_____

_____

_____

_____

BRAINSTORM
As many ideas as you can to help you have an impactful and successful project.

What I hope to gain from this project:

_____

_____

_____

_____

_____

_____

_____

A report of my project (including specifics of what I did and what I learned):

Knowledge Project

CHOICE & ACCOUNTABILITY

Fill this page with doodles of all the QUOTES and SCRIPTURES you can find about CHOICE & ACCOUNTABILITY. Be certain to include the saying about this value in your Personal Progress booklet.

As a Daughter of God
I Can Make Wise Decisions & Solve Problems

Study the following scriptures and doodle what they teach you.

1 Nephi 15:8

2 Nephi 32:3

Alma 34:19-27

Ether 2-3

D&C 9:7-9

102

Choice & Accountability #1

What are some small and large important choices that you are making at this stage in your life?

How would a regular pattern of prayer and scripture study help you in making these important choices?

 Make a plan on how you can improve your prayers and scripture study.

Choice & Accountability #1

Righteous

Read through your entire FOR THE STRENGTH OF YOUTH PAMPHLET. Every time you come across a specific standard of righteous behavior, doodle it on these pages.

Add your own thoughts about why those standards are important.

104

Behaviors

Choice & Accountability #2

3 Standards

From all of the standards you doodled, choose 3 that you could improve in. List them below.

1-

2-

3-

For three weeks strive to live those standards as best as you can. Each night report on how you did.

	DATE	WHAT I DID TO LIVE THE 3 STANDARDS
Day #1		
Day #2		
Day #3		
Day #4		
Day #5		
Day #6		
Day #7		
Day #8		

Choice & Accountability #2

Day #9		
Day #10		
Day #11		
Day #12		
Day #13		
Day #14		
Day #15		
Day #16		
Day #17		
Day #18		
Day #19		
Day #20		
Day #21		

Choice & Accountability #2

Review

What did you learn from this three week challenge to better live those three standards?

How was your life blessed while living those three standards?

How did your effort in living these standards bless others?

What are you going to change permanently because of this experience?

Choice & Accountability #2

AGENCY

Study about **AGENCY** in the following scriptures. Doodle what you learn all over this page.

Joshua 24:15

2 Nephi 2

D&C 82:2-10

Choice & Accountability #3

Ask a parent or important adult in your life to write you a letter about the blessings and responsibilities of agency. Ask them to give you advice and counsel on how to properly use the gift of agency.

Choice & Accountability #3

After you have studied the scriptures about "agency" and read the letter written to you, write a journal entry about your understanding of "agency" and how you should use this gift in your life.

Choice & Accountability #3

Repentance

Study about **REPENTANCE** in the following scriptures. Doodle what you learn all over this page.

Isaiah 1:18

Alma 26:22

Alma 34:30-35

Moroni 8:25-26

D&C 19:15-20

D&C 58:42-43

Choice & Accountability #4

Continue studying about **REPENTANCE** using your other resources such as you *For the Strength of Youth* pamphlet and *True to the Faith.* Doodle what you learn here.

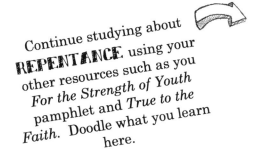

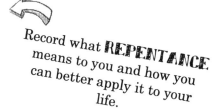

Record what **REPENTANCE** means to you and how you can better apply it to your life.

THE HOLY GHOST

Study about **THE HOLY GHOST** in the following scriptures. Doodle what you learn all over this page.

Ezekiel 36:26-27

John 14:26

John 16:13

Galatians 5:22-25

2 Nephi 32:5

Moroni 10:4-5

D&C 11:12-14

Continue studying about
THE HOLY GHOST using
your other resources such as
True to the Faith. Doodle
what you learn here.

Write about how the **HOLY GHOST** can help you make good choices every day.

The Young Women Theme

Study the YOUNG WOMEN THEME. Look for what the theme teaches you about the following things and doodle what you find.

Who I am

What I am to do

Why I am to do it

What I Will Do

Write what you will do each day in the following areas to remain **MORALLY CLEAN** and be worthy to enter the **TEMPLE.**

Modesty

Dating

Media

Wise Money Management

Study the following references and doodle what insights they give you about **CHOICES** and **WISE MONEY MANAGEMENT.**

Moses 4:1-4

Moses 7:32

2 Nephi 9:51

Work and Self-Reliance *(For the Strength of Youth)*

Budget

*Make and live by a budget for at least three months.

Month 1: _____

Projected Budget

How much money I think
I will make this month: _____

Fill out at the beginning of the month

Tithing: _____

Savings:

- College: _____
- Mission: _____
- Other:

Spending:

- Entertainment:_____
- Clothing:_____
- Car / Gas: _____
- School
  activities and
  necessities:_____
- Food: _____
- Gifts: _____
- Hobbies:_____
- Other:

Total: _____

This number should be the
same as the projected income.

Actual Budget

How much money I actually
made this month: _____

*Fill out at the end of the month with your
actual numbers.*

Tithing: _____

Savings:

- College: _____
- Mission: _____
- Other:

Spending:

- Entertainment:_____
- Clothing:_____
- Car / Gas: _____
- School
  activities and
  necessities: _____
- Food: _____
- Gifts:_____
- Hobbies:_____
- Other:

Total: _____

This number should be the
same as the actual income.

Choice & Accountability #7

Budget

Month 2: _____

Projected Budget

How much money I think
I will make this month: _____

Fill out at the beginning of the month

Tithing: _____

Savings:

- College: _____
- Mission: _____
- Other:

Spending:

- Entertainment:_____
- Clothing:_____
- Car / Gas: _____
- School activities and necessities:_____
- Food: _____
- Gifts: _____
- Hobbies: _____
- Other:

Total: _____

This number should be the
same as the projected income.

Actual Budget

How much money I actually
made this month: _____

Fill out at the end of the month with your actual numbers.

Tithing: _____

Savings:

- College: _____
- Mission: _____
- Other:

Spending:

- Entertainment:_____
- Clothing:_____
- Car / Gas: _____
- School activities and necessities: _____
- Food: _____
- Gifts:_____
- Hobbies:_____
- Other:

Total: _____

This number should be the
same as the actual income.

Choice & Accountability #7

Budget

* After two months of budgets, see how accurate you can be this month!

Month 3: _____

Projected Budget

How much money I think
I will make this month: _____

Fill out at the beginning of the month

Tithing: _____

Savings:

- College: _____
- Mission: _____
- Other:

Spending:

- Entertainment:_____
- Clothing:_____
- Car / Gas: _____
- School activities and necessities:_____
- Food: _____
- Gifts: _____
- Hobbies: _____
- Other:

Total: _____

This number should be the
same as the projected income.

Actual Budget

How much money I actually
made this month: _____

Fill out at the end of the month with your actual numbers.

Tithing: _____

Savings:

- College: _____
- Mission: _____
- Other:

Spending:

- Entertainment:_____
- Clothing:_____
- Car / Gas: _____
- School activities and necessities: _____
- Food: _____
- Gifts:_____
- Hobbies:_____
- Other:

Total: _____

This number should be the
same as the actual income.

Choice & Accountability #7

What did you learn from three months of keeping a budget?

_____
_____
_____
_____
_____
_____
_____
_____
_____

How will keeping and living by a budget bless you and your future family's life?

_____
_____
_____
_____
_____
_____
_____
_____
_____
_____
_____
_____
_____
_____
_____
_____
_____

Choice & Accountability #7

My Project

For my project I have chosen to:

_____
_____
_____
_____
_____
_____
_____

BRAINSTORM
As many ideas as you can to help you have an impactful and successful project.

What I hope to gain from this project:

_____
_____
_____
_____
_____
_____
_____

Choice & Accountability Project

A report of my project (including specifics of what I did and what I learned):

Choice & Accountability Project

GOOD WORKS

Fill this page with doodles of all the **QUOTES** and **SCRIPTURES** you can find about **GOOD WORKS**.
Be certain to include the saying about this value in your Personal Progress booklet.

Serving Others

Study these scriptures and then doodle what you learn about **WHY SERVICE IS SUCH AN IMPORTANT PART OF THE GOSPEL.**

Matthew 5:13-16

Matthew 25:34-40

Galatians 6:9-10

James 1:22-27

Mosiah 2:17

Mosiah 4:26

3 Nephi 13:1-4

We are surrounded by people who are constantly giving meaningful service. FOR TWO WEEKS, pay close attention to the SERVICE BEING DONE, ESPECIALLY IN YOUR FAMILY. Each night record what you witnessed that day.

Day 1 Date:	Day 2 Date:
_____	_____
_____	_____
_____	_____
_____	_____
_____	_____

Day 3 Date:	Day 4 Date:
_____	_____
_____	_____
_____	_____
_____	_____
_____	_____

Day 5 Date:	Day 6 Date:
_____	_____
_____	_____
_____	_____
_____	_____
_____	_____

Day 7 Date:	Day 8 Date:
_____	_____
_____	_____
_____	_____
_____	_____
_____	_____

Good Works #1

Day 9   Date:

_____
_____
_____
_____
_____

Day 10   Date:

_____
_____
_____
_____
_____

Day 11   Date:

_____
_____
_____
_____
_____

Day 12   Date:

_____
_____
_____
_____
_____

Day 13   Date:

_____
_____
_____
_____
_____

Day 14   Date:

_____
_____
_____
_____
_____

How did this experience impact you?

_____
_____
_____
_____
_____
_____
_____
_____

Good Works #1

FAMILY MEALS
Week 1: _____

FOR TWO WEEKS, help plan and make your **FAMILY MEALS.** Include planning the menus, getting the food and preparing it.

MENU

MONDAY
- Breakfast:
- Lunch:
- Snacks:
- Dinner:

TUESDAY
- Breakfast:
- Lunch:
- Snacks:
- Dinner:

WEDNESDAY
- Breakfast:
- Lunch:
- Snacks:
- Dinner:

THURSDAY
- Breakfast:
- Lunch:
- Snacks:
- Dinner:

FRIDAY
- Breakfast:
- Lunch:
- Snacks:
- Dinner:

SATURDAY
- Breakfast:
- Lunch:
- Snacks:
- Dinner:

SUNDAY
- Breakfast:
- Lunch:
- Snacks:
- Dinner:

GROCERY LIST

Good Works #2

FAMILY MEALS Week 2: _____

MENU

MONDAY

- Breakfast:
- Lunch:
- Snacks:
- Dinner:

TUESDAY

- Breakfast:
- Lunch:
- Snacks:
- Dinner:

WEDNESDAY

- Breakfast:
- Lunch:
- Snacks:
- Dinner:

THURSDAY

- Breakfast:
- Lunch:
- Snacks:
- Dinner:

FRIDAY

- Breakfast:
- Lunch:
- Snacks:
- Dinner:

SATURDAY

- Breakfast:
- Lunch:
- Snacks:
- Dinner:

SUNDAY

- Breakfast:
- Lunch:
- Snacks:
- Dinner:

GROCERY LIST

Good Works #2

Comforting Others
& Bearing Other's Burdens

 Doodle what **Mosiah 18:7-10** teaches you.

Brainstorm a bunch of ways that you can comfort others or help them bear their burdens. Be specific.

Pick 3 of the things that you thought of for how you can comfort another person. Do each of them and report about your experiences here.

1
_____
_____
_____
_____
_____
_____
_____

2
_____
_____
_____
_____
_____
_____
_____

3
_____
_____
_____
_____
_____
_____
_____

Good Works #3

SERVICE Family Home Evening

Teach a lesson on service to your family for Family Home Evening. Use the guide below to help plan it.

SCRIPTURES I WOULD LIKE TO USE:

A fun idea to get my family excited for the lesson (something I can do earlier in the day or week):	A good way to introduce the lesson (a good story, object lesson, video, etc.):
What points I would like to teach, and how I can teach them :	What we can do as a family because of what we have learned about service:

133

Good Works #4

Serving Family

Study
D&C 58:26-28
Doodle what these
scriptures teach you.

Pick a family member...

and make a serious effort of serving them for an entire month. Come to this page every night and doodle what you did to serve them. Include your feelings and how your service is impacting your relationship with this person.

Serving Outside of Your Family

Spend at least **THREE** **HOURS** serving people outside of your family. Doodle here your experiences, including their reaction, how you felt, and future goals for continued service.

Missionary Experience

Through your example and good works, others will want to know more about the Gospel. Study these scriptures and doodle what they teach you about this:

Matthew 24:14

Matthew 28:19

D&C 88:81

Good Works #7

Pray for a missionary experience and as you feel inspired, invite a friend who is not a member or is less active, to church or an activity. Write about your experience here.

Good Works #7

My Project

For my project I have chosen to:

_____

_____

_____

_____

_____

_____

BRAINSTORM
As many ideas as you can to help you have an impactful and successful project.

What I hope to gain from this project:

_____

_____

_____

_____

_____

_____

A report of my project (including specifics of what I did and what I learned):

Good Works Project

INTEGRITY

Fill this page with doodles of all the **QUOTES** and **SCRIPTURES** you can find about **INTEGRITY.** Be certain to include the saying about this value in your Personal Progress booklet.

Integrity

Doodle the
DEFINITION OF INTEGRITY.
Include the description in your Personal Progress book on value experience #1.

Read
MORONI 10:30-33.
Doodle what you learn from those verses.

What do you think it means to **"Deny yourselves of all ungodliness"** as taught in Moroni 10:32?

Living What I Believe

One definition of "Integrity" is *the state of being whole; undivided.* So if you have integrity you "wholly" or completely live what you say you believe.

Search through your *For the Strength of Youth* pamphlet looking for any counsel you can about the following things. Doodle what you find in the appropriate boxes.

HOW I SHOULD BEHAVE	HOW I SHOULD DRESS	MY CONVERSATIONS
LITERATURE / BOOKS	MOVIES / TELEVISION	INTERNET
MUSIC	CELL PHONES	OTHER MEDIA

143

Integrity #1

One Month Challenge:

For one month do all you can to live these standards with great integrity. Each night review your day and consider your choices in comparison with the standards you filled in on the last page. If you feel you had integrity in that standard, mark the box. Start by filling in one month of dates in the left column, starting with tomorrow's date.

Date	Behavior	Dress	Conversations	Books	Movies/TV	Internet	Music	Cell Phones	Media

Integrity #1

Review of Challenge:

How did making such a concentrated effort of fully living those standards impact your life?

What did you learn about what it means to have integrity?

What efforts are you going to continue to make in your life to remain virtuous and be worthy of the temple?

Integrity #1

MY INTEGRITY
Self-Assessment

Consider the following questions and do an honest self-assessment on each of them.

Do I avoid gossip?

_____
_____
_____
_____
_____
_____
_____

Do I avoid inappropriate jokes?

_____
_____
_____
_____
_____
_____
_____
_____
_____

Do I avoid swearing and profanity?

_____
_____
_____
_____
_____
_____
_____

Am I ever light minded about sacred subjects?

_____
_____
_____
_____
_____
_____
_____

Am I completely truthful?

_____
_____
_____
_____
_____
_____
_____
_____

Am I completely morally clean?

_____
_____
_____
_____
_____
_____
_____

Integrity #2

Am I honest in all things?

_____

_____

_____

_____

_____

_____

_____

Am I dependable?

_____

_____

_____

_____

_____

_____

_____

Am I trustworthy in my schoolwork?

_____

_____

_____

_____

_____

_____

_____

Am I trustworthy in all of my activities?

_____

_____

_____

_____

_____

_____

_____

After doing this self-assessment what can you do to improve YOUR PERSONAL INTEGRITY?

What is one NEW HABIT that you would like to improve?

Integrity #2

EXAMPLES of Integrity

Read about the following people in the scriptures. Doodle what they teach you about **INTEGRITY** in those scriptures.

JESUS CHRIST
3 Nephi 11:10-11

JOSEPH OF EGYPT
Genesis 39

ESTHER
The Book of Esther

SHADRACH, MESHACH, & ABED-NEGO
Daniel 3

DANIEL
Daniel 6

JOB
Job 2:3 and 27:3-6

PAUL
Acts 26

HYRUM SMITH
D&C 124:15

JOSEPH SMITH
Joseph Smith History 1:21-25

Integrity #3

Doodle about some times when you have been an example of

INTEGRITY,

especially when it was unpopular or hard.

149

Integrity #3

INTERVIEW

Interview your mother, grandmother or another important woman in your life about her understanding of the importance of

INTEGRITY,

Doodle questions you could ask her and then record her answers next to your questions.

Doodle
A LIST OF IDEAS
of how you can make your choices and actions consistent with what you know is right and wrong.

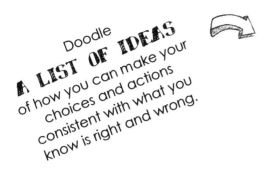

After everything you have studied, done and learned, <u>what does it mean to you to have</u> **INTEGRITY?**

STANDING AS A WITNESS

Doodle the scripture (word for word) **MOSIAH 18:9** on this page.

How can you STAND AS A WITNESS OF GOD AT ALL TIMES, THINGS AND PLACES?

Choose a behavior that you can improve so you can be a better example of standing as a witness of God at all times, things and places. Write the behavior you would like to work on in this box:

For three weeks work on improving that behavior. Practice integrity by being honest with yourself as you seek to become better and stronger. Each night evaluate how you did that day.

DAY 1 ⇨
Date:

DAY 2 ⇨
Date:

DAY 3 ⇨
Date:

DAY 4 ⇨
Date:

DAY 5 ⇨
Date:

Integrity #5

DAY 6 ⇨
Date:

DAY 7 ⇨
Date:

DAY 8 ⇨
Date:

DAY 9 ⇨
Date:

DAY 10 ⇨
Date:

DAY 11 ⇨
Date:

DAY 12 ⇨
Date:

DAY 13 ⇨
Date:

Integrity #5

DAY 14 ⇨
Date:

DAY 15 ⇨
Date:

DAY 16 ⇨
Date:

DAY 17 ⇨
Date:

DAY 18 ⇨
Date:

DAY 19 ⇨
Date:

DAY 20 ⇨
Date:

DAY 21 ⇨
Date:

Integrity in FASTING

Look up **"FASTING AND FAST OFFERINGS"** in True to the Faith. Study the entire description. Doodle what you learn on this page.

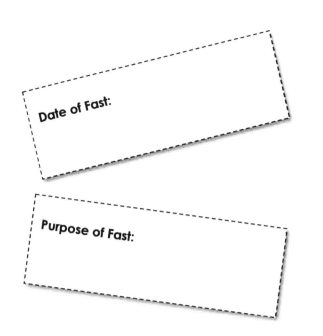

Date of Fast:

Purpose of Fast:

On a
FAST SUNDAY,
Fast as perfectly as possible, using the knowledge you gained on the last page. Record your experience on this page.

STRENGTHENING FAMILY

List all of the
ISSUES
TRENDS
& PROBLEMS
that you can think of that
are weakening the family.

Integrity #7

Read the following things and doodle on the page what they teach you about

HOW YOU CAN STRENGTHEN FAMILIES

- **The First Presidency Message on page 1 of your Personal Progress book.**
- **The Family: A Proclamation to the World.**
- **"Family" in *For the Strength of Youth***

STRENGTHENING FAMILY
Quotes

Search through Church magazines or on www.lds.org for counsel the leaders of the Church have given to us about **STRENGTHENING THE FAMILY.** Doodle them here.

What are your plans and ideas to strengthen your family?

What efforts are you making right now to prepare to have a strong family of your own?

What values and traditions do you want to establish in your future family?

Integrity #7

My Project

For my project I have chosen to:

_____

_____

_____

_____

_____

_____

_____

BRAINSTORM
As many ideas as you can to help you have an impactful and successful project.

What I hope to gain from this project:

_____

_____

_____

_____

_____

_____

_____

A report of my project (including specifics of what I did and what I learned):

Integrity Project

VIRTUE

Fill this page with doodles of all the **QUOTES** and **SCRIPTURES** you can find about **VIRTUE.**   Be certain to include the saying about this value in your Personal Progress booklet.

Promised Blessings

Virtue experience #1
in your Personal
Progress book.

Moroni 9:9

Jacob 2:28

"The Family: a
Proclamation to the
World"

"Sexual Purity" in *For
the Strength of Youth*

Article of Faith #13

Proverbs 31:10-31

Study the importance of
CHASTITY &
VIRTUE
by reading the following
references. Doodle what
you learn on these two
pages.

of being *sexually pure*

What are your promised blessings for being sexually pure?

_____

_____

_____

_____

_____

_____

_____

_____

_____

_____

_____

_____

_____

What is your personal commitment to be sexually pure?

_____

_____

_____

_____

_____

_____

_____

_____

_____

_____

_____

_____

_____

_____

_____

Virtue #1

VIRTUOUS LIVING
and *the Holy Ghost*

Study the relationship between

BEING VIRTUOUS AND THE COMPANIONSHIP OF THE HOLY GHOST

by reading the following references. Doodle what you learn on this page.

Virtue experience #2 in your Personal Progress book.

John 14:26-27

John 15:26

2 Nephi 32:1-5

D&C 45:57-59

D&C 88:3-4

D&C 121:45-46

What have you learned about the relationship between being virtuous and being guided by the Holy Ghost?

Record some times that you have felt guided by the Holy Ghost.

Virtue #2

Preparing to enter the
TEMPLE

Study
ALMA 5
And in the left column write all of the questions that Alma asks, and in the right column write your personal answers to the questions.

Virtue #3

Doodle **A LIST** of **THINGS YOU CAN DO** to prepare yourself to be pure and worthy to enter the temple and receive the blessings waiting for you there. Think of as many things as possible.

Virtue #3

REPENTANCE

Study about
REPENTANCE
by reading the following
references. Doodle what
you learn on this page.

Virtue experience #4
in your Personal
Progress book.

Moroni 10:32-33

The Book of Enos

"Repentance" in *For
the Strength of Youth*

D&C 20:77

D&C 20:79

Why is repentance such a blessing?

What can you do to be and remain pure and worthy?

What can you do to make partaking of the Sacrament more meaningful and bring spiritual power into your life?

Virtue #4

My Virtue Project

As you STUDY THE BOOK OF MORMON use the following pages to doodle the following things:

- Favorite phrases
- Favorite scriptures
- Things you have learned
- Personal thoughts
- Pictures
- Stories
- Diagrams
- Etc.

1 Nephi 1-4

1 Nephi 5-7

1 Nephi 8

1 Nephi 9-10

1 Nephi 11-12

Virtue Project

1 Nephi 13-14

1 Nephi 15-18

1 Nephi 19-22

2 Nephi 1-2

2 Nephi 3-7

2 Nephi 8-10

2 Nephi 11-15

2 Nephi 16-19

2 Nephi 20-24

2 Nephi 25-27

2 Nephi 28-30

2 Nephi 31-32

JACOB 1-4

JACOB 5

JACOB 6-7

ENOS

JAROM -
OMNI

WORDS OF MORMON

Mosiah 1-3

Mosiah 4-6

Virtue Project

Mosiah 7-8

Mosiah 9-11

Mosiah 12-14

Mosiah 15-16

Virtue Project

Mosiah 17-18

Mosiah 19-22

Mosiah 23-25

Virtue Project

Mosiah 26-29

ALMA 1-4

ALMA 5-6

ALMA 7-8

ALMA 9-11

ALMA 12-16

ALMA 17-21

ALMA 22-25

ALMA 26-29

ALMA 30-32

ALMA 33-35

ALMA 36-37

ALMA 38

ALMA 39-42

ALMA 43-44

ALMA 45-46

ALMA 47-49

ALMA 50-52

226

Virtue Project

ALMA 53-55

ALMA 56-57

ALMA 58-61

Virtue Project

ALMA 62-63

Helaman 1-4

Helaman 5-7

Helaman 8-12

Helaman 13-16

3 Nephi 1-3

3 Nephi 4-6

Virtue Project

3 Nephi 7-8

Virtue Project

Virtue Project

3 Nephi 12-13

Virtue Project

3 Nephi 14-15

3 Nephi 16-18

3 Nephi 19-20

3 Nephi 21-23

Virtue Project

Virtue Project

4 NEPHI 1

Mormon 1-3

Mormon 4-6

Mormon 7-9

ETHER 1-2

ETHER 3

ETHER 4-6

Ether 7-8

Ether 9-12

Virtue Project

Ether 13-15

Virtue Project

Moroni 1-5

Moroni 6

Moroni 7

Moroni 8-9

Moroni 10

Did your study of the Book of Mormon bring increased power into your life to resist temptation? What specific things did you notice?

Did you notice increased spirituality?

Virtue Project

What were some specific scriptures and stories that had an impact on you?

_____
_____
_____
_____
_____
_____
_____
_____
_____
_____
_____
_____
_____
_____
_____
_____
_____
_____
_____
_____
_____
_____
_____
_____
_____
_____
_____

What is your personal testimony of the Book of Mormon?

Virtue Project

61460560R00147

Made in the USA
Lexington, KY
10 March 2017